WRITING PROMPTS FOR KIDS

WRITING PROMPTS for Kids

A Creative Workbook for Ages 7 to 9

Emily Aierstok

ROCKRIDGE PRESS

**To Kevin, Ava, Max, and Cam:
Thank you for giving me a
world full of beautiful stories.**

First Rockridge Press trade paperback edition 2022

Rockridge Press and the Rockridge Press logo are trademarks or registered trademarks of Callisto Media Inc. and/or its affiliates in the United States and other countries and may not be used without written permission.

For general information on our other products and services, please contact our Customer Care Department within the United States at (866) 744-2665, or outside the United States at (510) 253-0500.

Paperback ISBN: 978-1-68539-571-1 | eBook ISBN: 978-1-68539-809-5

Manufactured in the United States of America

Interior and Cover Designer: Michael Cook and Joshua Moore
Art Producer: Hannah Dickerson
Editor: Maxine Marshall
Production Editor: Ruth Sakata Corley
Production Manager: Jose Olivera

All illustrations used under license from Shutterstock.com and iStock.com, except for the following:
© Robin Boyer, p. 47; © Collaborate Agency, p. 58
Author photo courtesy of Stephanie Challis Photography

10 9 8 7 6 5 4 3 2 1 0

Contents

Introduction

Imagine waking up in a candy castle. Your bed is a marshmallow. The lamps around you are made of lollipops. The door is a giant chocolate bar. You are suddenly in an amazing story!

This book is designed to help you explore **narrative writing**. Narrative is another word for story. I have been teaching kids how to bring stories to life for over twenty years. I am a teacher and a mom of three awesome kids. My kids and I love telling stories, especially the ones we create ourselves.

Writing allows you to find your voice. No one can tell the stories from your imagination except YOU. Your stories matter! You might make mistakes along the way, but that's okay. Have an eraser nearby as you work through the book. If you use your eraser a lot, it just means you are writing like an author. Keep trying, and have fun!

Remember, stories can take you anywhere, from candy castles to riding on the back of a tiger. Where will your stories take you?

How to Use This Book

This book is divided into three parts. In part 1, you'll learn how to start a super story that will get your readers hooked. Prompts in part 1 will help you brainstorm ideas for stories, collect awesome words to include in your stories, and more. Then, in part 2, you'll fill the middle of your story with interesting characters, the perfect **setting**, and events that will keep your readers on the edge of their seats. There are prompts to explore why the characters in a story do the things they do, and to practice using all the five senses to create settings that feel real. Finally, in part 3, you will learn how to write an ending that will WOW your readers. You'll practice checking your writing for mistakes and imagine how different endings can change a story.

There are lots of steps to creating a great story! Don't worry, you don't have to learn everything all at once. You have already learned new words: narrative writing!

New vocabulary words are bolded the first time that they appear. When you see a bolded word, know that

you can always flip to the glossary on page 94 to see a definition.

It's easiest to go through the book from beginning to end. But remember, the stories are yours to build. Feel free to skip around if you have an awesome idea.

There are three sections in the book called "My Ideas." Use that space to write, draw, collect, hide snacks, or grow new ideas so that you don't lose track of them. Let's get writing! Before you dive in to part 1, fill out the next page to start your journey as a writer.

My Story

_____'s Writing Book

The stories in this book are:

☐ for the world to see. ☐ just for me.

My very best writing ideas come from _____

_____.

If I could write anywhere in the world, I would write while:

☐ sitting on a cloud. ☐ riding an elephant.

☐ in my closet with all of ☐ _____
my stuffed animals.

I believe in myself as a writer because:

1. my imagination is powerful.

2. my stories are important.

3. _____.

I can't wait to write!

PART 1

Ready, Set, Go!

What makes a story special? YOU. You are the only person who can tell the stories from your imagination. In this section, you are going to focus on getting your ideas on paper and starting a story. The ideas might seem silly at first. It might seem hard to find the right words, but that's okay. Free your ideas. See what kind of magic happens!

Time to Brainstorm

Ideas swirling around in your brain might feel messy like a storm. They might float like feathers in the wind or hide under a rock. The prompts in this section will help you grab hold of your ideas and write them down. Brainstorming is the first step of writing a story. Write your ideas on paper so you will never lose them. This book will get you started! Remember, you can always flip to the "My Ideas" sections and write or draw ideas for your stories.

If you feel stuck staring at a blank page, don't worry. There are lots of tricks that writers use to get started. You can walk away and come back later. You can read a favorite story to spark your imagination.

You can also try **freewriting**. Freewriting means you write whatever is in your brain. Set a timer for one, two, or three minutes. Write without stopping until the timer goes off. Don't worry about spelling, grammar, or punctuation. You don't even have to make complete sentences. When you're done, look through your thoughts on paper and see if you can find a writing idea. It's like finding buried treasure!

Visiting My Imagination

Imagine you are a visitor from the future. You have just landed on Earth and it's nighttime. But that's okay—you have special nighttime vision! What does this moment **look, smell, sound, and feel** like? Write down all the details you think you would notice.

_____

_____

_____

_____

_____

_____

_____

_____

_____

_____

_____

_____

_____

Starting a New Story

Getting started with a new story can be hard. Try these tips to help: draw your ideas, make a list, write without stopping until you fill a space, or collect inspiration from the world around you. Test out the tips here, then draw a star next to the tips that helped the most.

▶ **Draw your ideas**

▶ **Make a list**

▶ **Write without stopping**

▶ **Collect inspiration (stickers, pictures, or words)**

Learning from Other Writers

When you are searching for ideas for your next story, it can be fun to take inspiration from other writers. Give it a try! List a few stories and their first sentences. You might notice that your favorite stories start with a description of a problem. Or, maybe they tell something about a character. Remember, never copy someone else's words. Let their words inspire you to write your own!

Story Title	First Sentence

Wonderful Words

Some words make cool sounds, like SPLAT or FIZZ! Some words feel more interesting or specific than others that mean the same thing. For example, instead of saying that two people are working together, you can say they are in CAHOOTS. Isn't that more fun?

Fill in this page with words you like. You don't have to make the whole list right now. When you see a word you like in a book or hear someone say it, jot it down here. Then, you'll know where to look when you are writing and you need a juicy word to use.

_____   _____

_____   _____

_____   _____

_____   _____

_____   _____

_____   _____

_____   _____

_____   _____

_____   _____

Drawing a Mind Map

Mind maps can help with brainstorming by showing us how ideas are connected. Fill in this mind map to brainstorm new story ideas. First, write your name in the big circle. Next, write four of your favorite things in the smaller circles, and record details about each of those things in the connecting boxes. Use these items and descriptions to help you spark a story idea.

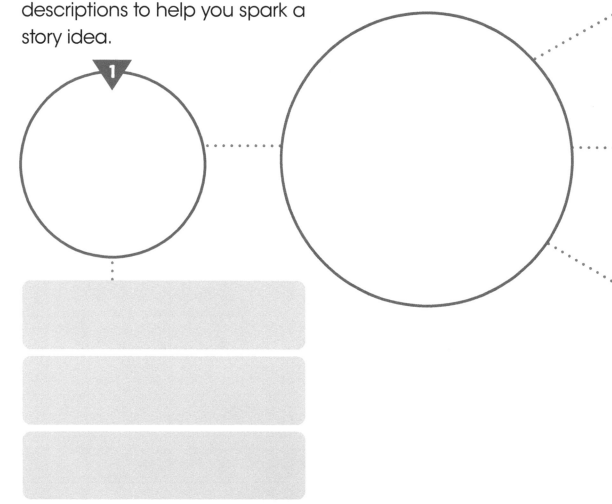

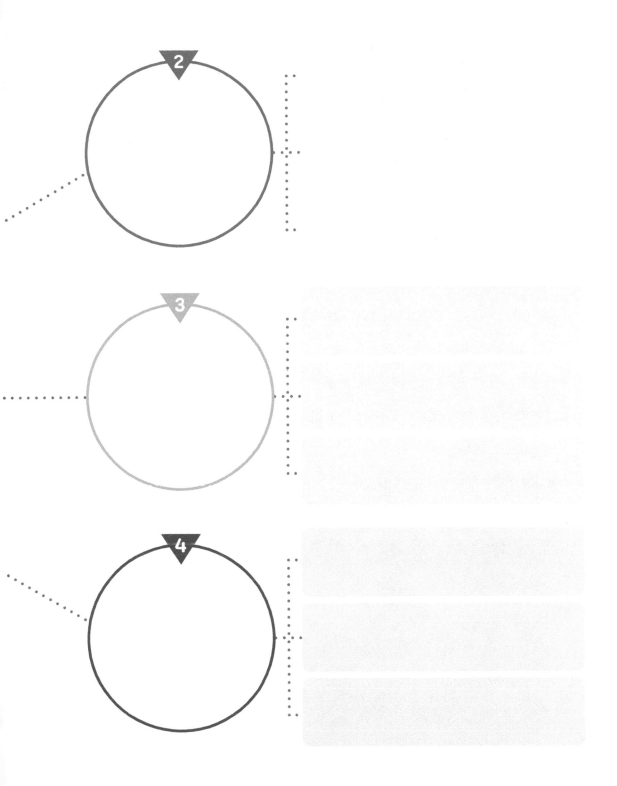

Incredible Ideas

Read through this list of writing ideas. Check off the ideas you would have fun writing about.

- ☐ A friendly *T. rex*
- ☐ A talkative tree
- ☐ A mermaid with a pirate best friend
- ☐ A scary *Brontosaurus*
- ☐ A snake who teaches a powerful lesson
- ☐ A story inspired by your favorite movie
- ☐ A story inspired by your favorite song
- ☐ Dragons who can't breathe fire
- ☐ Magical flowers
- ☐ Making the winning shot
- ☐ Saving a melting snowman
- ☐ Skiing down a mountain
- ☐ The life story of a bug
- ☐ The smell of cookies

Starting Your Stories

Have you ever been fishing? The goal of fishing is to hook a fish and reel it in. The goal of the beginning of your story is the same, except you want to hook a reader instead of a fish! There are great ways to start a story and the prompts in this section will help get you there! You'll learn how to fill the beginning of your stories with energy, using action words called **verbs**. Starting a story in the middle of an exciting scene is called an **action lead**.

Each time you start a story, you'll want to decide which character is telling the story. The prompts in this section will help you think about **point of view**. Point of view is when a character tells a story through their own personal experiences.

Exciting Verbs

Using powerful action words at the beginning of a story can get readers excited. Think of superheroes who run, jump, and fly through the sky. *Run, jump,* and *fly* are all action words called verbs.

Write a list of action words that you might use to start a story. You don't have to fill in the whole list all at once. When you hear a fun action word, flip to this page and write it down!

_____ _____

_____ _____

_____ _____

_____ _____

_____ _____

_____ _____

_____ _____

_____ _____

_____ _____

_____ _____

_____ _____

Jumping in with Action Leads

The world's oldest superhero just came to town! Try writing an action lead. That means you start a story in the middle of an exciting action scene. Some action words to try: *swooped, glared, zipped, zapped,* and *soared.*

_____

_____

_____

_____

_____

_____

_____

_____

_____

_____

_____

_____

_____

_____

Writing Secrets

Set up the perfect writing space—a quiet place where you can let your creativity flow without interruptions. Here are some things that might help you stay focused and inspired:

▶ **Your favorite stuffed animals.** They can give you ideas or support. You might even choose to write a story as if they were talking.

▶ **A soft pillow and blanket** so you can get cozy.

▶ **Fun pens, pencils, and this writing book,** plus a few of your favorite books to turn to for ideas.

▶ **A snack** and/or a glass of water for when you need a writing break.

▶ **Your imagination.** Luckily, that comes with you wherever you go!

Start with a Conversation

Starting a story with a conversation between two characters is a fun way to introduce them to the reader. Imagine you are starting a story where a tiger is having a friendly chat with a mouse. Use the word bubbles to show what they say.

The Flower Said to the Bee

Starting a story with two characters talking can get the reader interested in their problems. Pretend you are listening to a chat between a flower and a bee. Fill in the blanks below to complete what they say to each other.

"Bee, your buzzing is so loud. Please _____

_____ ,"

said the flower.

The bee looked _____

_____ and

responded, "_____ ."

This made the flower feel _____

_____ .

The flower shouted / sniffled / whispered (circle one),

"_____

_____ ."

Point of View

To begin a story, you will need to decide which character is telling the story. To practice, pick a member of your family and start a story from their point of view. That means you get to pretend you are seeing the world through that person's eyes. What would you see?

_____

_____

_____

_____

_____

_____

_____

_____

_____

_____

_____

_____

_____

My Ideas

Get creative—write, draw, and paste ideas here!

PART 2

Who, What, Where, When, Why?

Now it's time to learn how to add the right ingredients to the middle of your story. Of course, no good recipe would be complete without a little spice. The "spices" of writing are details and descriptions. The prompts in this section will help you cook up an amazing story by adding interesting characters, exciting events, and a detailed setting.

What a Character!

Stories usually have at least one main character who readers get to know best. The main character is sometimes called a **hero**. The opposite of a hero is a **villain**. Your characters can be people, animals, aliens, or any other creatures, real or imagined. A superhero snail? Sounds cool. A pickle who sings in a band? Awesome.

The prompts in this section will help you write characters who seem real, even if they are aliens! You will learn to use **nouns** and **adjectives** to describe your character's looks. You will use **verbs** to describe their actions. You'll also explore fun ways to show what the character says and what others say about them. This is called **dialogue**. Dialogue allows readers to listen to what your characters are saying. Last, you can show a character's thoughts. Let your reader sneak inside your character's head. Let's write some characters!

Name Game

When you are writing a new character, you can start by choosing their name. Use this page to write a list of cool names that you could use for your characters. You can come back and fill in this list as you hear names you like. You don't have to come up with a whole list right now!

_____   _____

_____   _____

_____   _____

_____   _____

_____   _____

_____   _____

_____   _____

_____   _____

_____   _____

_____   _____

_____   _____

Inspiring Ideas for New Characters

Many writers imagine characters that are like people they know. That's a great trick to help you get started! Paste or draw pictures here of people who inspire you. Challenge yourself to write about characters inspired by the pictures in your collage.

Brainstorming Characters

Brainstorming different descriptions for characters is a fun way to start imagining! Read through the lists. Check off things you are interested in using to create characters you won't forget. Then, next time you are starting a new story, you can flip back to this page for some cool character ideas.

LOOKS

- ☐ Colorful
- ☐ Furry
- ☐ Scruffy
- ☐ Short
- ☐ Tall

ACTIONS

- ☐ Driving
- ☐ Planning
- ☐ Running
- ☐ Snoring
- ☐ Swimming

SIDEKICKS

- ☐ Astronaut
- ☐ Athlete
- ☐ Beetle
- ☐ Mouse
- ☐ Post office worker

QUIRKS

- ☐ Always late
- ☐ Extra loud
- ☐ Extra quiet
- ☐ Forgetful
- ☐ Messy

Freewriting a Character

Read through the character qualities you checked off on page 24. Use them to create a character. Freewrite your ideas until this page is full. Remember, freewriting means you write without stopping. Just get your ideas on the page and have fun!

_____

_____

_____

_____

_____

_____

_____

_____

_____

_____

_____

_____

_____

Describing Characters

Let's practice describing your characters to make them feel real. Draw a line matching a descriptive word (called an adjective) on the left with a noun on the right.

ADJECTIVES	NOUNS
Brainy	Butterfly
Silly	Mermaid
Sparkling	Pickle
Wild	Rock Star

Now, draw a silly character inspired by your matchup.

Creating a Hero

The hero of a story is the main character. Practice writing a hero by circling the character idea you like best, then make the character feel real by describing their thoughts, feelings, and actions.

CHARACTER IDEAS:

► A beautiful head of broccoli

► A kind *T. rex*

► An old stuffed animal

My character's name is _____.

My character wants _____.

My character thinks _____.

My character feels _____.

My character hopes _____.

My character loves _____.

My character's biggest mistake is _____

_____.

My character likes to eat _____.

The Vicious Vegetable Strikes Again!

In a story, the villain is against the hero. Describe your villains with lots of detail to make them feel real. Your villains can be as silly or as scary as you want. Give it a try! Make up a vegetable villain, then write about them for one minute without stopping. Describe the vegetable's looks, actions, words, thoughts, and feelings.

_____

_____

_____

_____

_____

_____

_____

_____

_____

_____

_____

_____

_____

What Is the Character Thinking?

When you are writing about your characters, imagine that you will let readers take a peek inside their head. Writing about your characters' thoughts will make them feel more real. Practice writing a character's thoughts by finishing each sentence to explain the reason for each action.

The dog barked out the window because

_____.

The librarian did story time outside because

_____.

The aliens crashed their spaceship when

_____.

The lobster snapped his claws because

_____.

The basketball player missed the shot when she saw

_____.

Writing Secrets

Great stories are full of imaginary characters who seem like they are alive. Try these tips to make robots, bugs, aliens, and even human characters seem more real.

▶ **Give characters a flaw.** No one is perfect. Maybe your robot is a hero, but he's known for returning his library books late. Flaws make characters seem real.

▶ **Share details about a character's life.** Does the robot love his mom? Does he always fight with his brother about who gets the last fruit bar? Little details can go a long way.

▶ **Add friends.** Every character has a good sidekick who cheers them on.

Get inspiration for your characters from the world around you. Family members, friends, teachers, classmates, and community members provide great ideas for characters.

Thinking Like Cats and Dogs

Characters feel more real to us when we know what they are thinking. A character's thoughts are called their point of view. The same story can be very different when told from different characters' points of view.

Let's experiment. Cats and dogs don't usually get along. Write one story from a cat's point of view. Then, write the same story from a dog's point of view.

Cat's point of view

Dog's point of view

Dragon Dialogue

When characters speak to each other in a story, it is called dialogue. Dialogue is a useful way to show what your characters want and think. Let's practice! A dragon burns down a sheep's house. He feels bad and wants to help the sheep rebuild. Use the word bubbles to show what the characters say to each other.

The Main Events

Now it's time to practice writing about the events in your story. Events in a story are called the **plot**. A plot has a beginning, middle, and end. A strong plot includes events that make readers excited to see what happens.

In the beginning of a story, you meet the characters. Then, a problem happens. This is called the **conflict**. Conflicts get in a character's way and make the story exciting. Then, **tension** builds. Tension is the edge-of-your-seat feeling that makes the reader wonder what will happen next.

In the middle of a story, everything might seem to be going wrong for the character. Luckily, there is usually a **turning point** where things start to fall into place. The last part of the plot happens when the character's problems are solved.

The prompts in this section will help you practice writing stories that build to exciting events and have thrilling turning points. The events in your stories can also help you share your message with the world. Some of these prompts will explore **theme**, which is the message that a story tells. Let's give it a try!

Noticing Great Plots

To practice writing stories with great plot structure, notice the plots of stories that you love. What is the plot of your favorite movie? Use the chart below to map out the events.

Movie: _____

Event one	
Event two	

Characters face their biggest challenge	
Turning point	
The problem is solved	

Climbing Plot Mountain

Add details to the story plot below by describing the **sights, sounds, smells, feels, and tastes** of each scene. As you write, pay attention to how the events build tension for the reader.

▶ **Event One:** A house cat named Bernie decides to escape to the great outdoors.

▶ **Event Two:** Bernie scurries up a mountain.

▶ **Event Three:** Bernie is lost.

▶ **Event Four (the turning point):** A mountain lion named Smokey helps Bernie to safety.

▶ **Event Five:** Bernie sits on his porch. His owners open the door. He is home.

Plot Mix-Up

Oh no! The events in a story have been scrambled. Remember that the order of events in a story is called the plot. Practice building exciting plots by putting the events in an order that makes sense. Number the events from 1 to 5.

_____ The spy runs after Cam. She stops him at the door.

_____ You overhear a classmate talking into her watch. She is a spy! She has discovered someone in your class is an alien.

_____ Cam explains that he is an alien from a planet made of food. He has chicken nuggets for everyone.

_____ The spy walks over to you. She shows you a picture of another classmate. It's your friend, Cam.

_____ Cam starts running for the door! You notice his hands are turning green.

ANSWER: 4, 1, 5, 2, 3

Three Kinds of Conflict

The problem in a story is called a conflict. Sometimes, conflicts are problems between two characters, like when two characters fight. In other stories, the conflict can be a problem in the world, like when a character is trying to solve a mystery. A third kind of conflict happens when a character has a problem inside their own thoughts, like when a character is afraid of something they must do. Practice imagining exciting conflicts for your stories by brainstorming three different conflicts a pirate might face.

Conflict with another character:

_____

_____

Conflict with the world around them:

_____

_____

Conflict with their thoughts and feelings:

_____

_____

The Plot of the Big Game

Now it is your turn to write a story with a great plot!
Imagine you are a famous _____
(fill in your favorite sport) player. Your team is down by one.
Write about the moment you score the game-winning
point / goal / home run   *(circle one)*.

_____

_____

_____

_____

_____

_____

_____

_____

_____

_____

_____

_____

Writing Secrets

Plan stories using a plot line shaped like a mountain. Try it out! Flip to the "My Ideas" section on page 72 and draw a mountain with steep sides and a peak, like an upside-down triangle.

▶ Start your plot line by brainstorming an event to introduce characters.

▶ As you move up the plot line mountain, brainstorm two or three events that happen to the characters.

▶ Right before reaching the top of the mountain, brainstorm an event that gives your character their biggest challenge. This will help to build tension.

▶ The top of the plot line is the turning point. Here, brainstorm how the character will start to work out their problem.

▶ Move down the plot line by brainstorming how your story will end.

Follow your plot line like a map. Remember, you can always change your ideas as you go.

Drawing the Plot

Drawing out a story can help you think about the plot structure. Give it a try! Use the spaces to draw the plot for a new story from your imagination.

Introduce the characters

Rising action

Rising action

Character's biggest challenge

Turning point

The problem is solved

Tremendous Turning Points

The turning point in a story happens when things start to get figured out. Brainstorm the turning point for each of the following stories:

Penelope and her best friend try out for the soccer team, but only Penelope makes it. They are both sad. Things get better when . . .

_____

_____

Max is hiding an alien from outer space in his locker. He's afraid someone will find out! Things get better when . . .

_____

_____

A family of rabbits has lived in a magical forest for centuries. They hear bulldozers in the distance. The rabbits are worried. Things get better when . . .

_____

_____

Plot Twist!

Many great stories are full of tension and surprising turning points. Imagine a suprising turning point here. Write the story of a bee who goes out into the world for the first time. Once she flies beyond her hive, she decides NOT to sting others.

_____

_____

_____

_____

_____

_____

_____

_____

_____

_____

_____

_____

My Message

Many stories include a message that the writer wants to share with readers. The message is called the theme, and it is always a complete idea. The message and the events in the plot are connected—the events in the story show how the message is true. It is your turn to think about messages that you might like to share in your stories! Read the list of common messages, then brainstorm your own.

COMMON MESSAGES IN A STORY:

▶ Be kind.

▶ Family comes first.

▶ Friendships are forever.

▶ Hard work pays off.

▶ Never give up.

MY MESSAGES:

1. _____

2. _____

3. _____

4. _____

5. _____

Be Yourself

The events in a story show how the theme, or the message, is true. For example, in a story with the message *never give up*, the events in the story will show a character trying hard even when they want to quit.

When you have a message you'd like to share in a story, brainstorm events that will show how that message is true. Try it here! Fill in the thought bubbles to brainstorm a superhero story based on the message *be yourself*.

Where Are We?

The setting of a story is where and when it happens. A setting could be a school in the 2000s, a castle in the 1700s, or a spaceship in the future.

When you write, bring your reader into the setting and let them experience it. Is the school warm and welcoming? Is the castle dark and evil? Is the spaceship smart and speedy? Bring your reader into the setting by describing the sights, sounds, smells, feels, and tastes. The prompts in this section will help you imagine interesting settings and paint a picture with descriptive words.

Setting also creates a **mood**. Mood is the way the story makes the reader feel. A dark cave full of screeching bats might make a reader feel scared. Writing about a world full of fluffy clouds, rainbows, and sunshine might make a reader feel happy. The prompts in this section will also help you think of what mood you want to create. Then, write a setting that fits.

Settings for My Stories

The setting is where and when a story happens. Stories can happen in different places and different times. Imagining a cool setting is a great way to start a story! Use this page to collect ideas for settings. Draw or glue pictures here. Then, come back to this page when you need inspiration for a great story setting.

Ready, Setting, Go!

Different settings are a better match for different stories. For example, it might be silly (but fun!) to write about people planting flowers on the moon. Use the table below to make lists of possible settings for different types of stories. When you are starting a new story, you can flip back to this page for ideas.

Sports settings	
Out-of-this-world settings	
Realistic settings	

Fantasy settings

Nature settings

Historical settings

Setting in the Sky

The settings in your stories will feel more real if they are full of details! Practice writing a setting here. Close your eyes and think of a castle in the clouds. Can you describe it so other people can imagine the place the way you do? Describe the **sights, sounds, smells, feels, and tastes.**

_____

_____

_____

_____

_____

_____

_____

_____

_____

_____

_____

Wish You Were Here

Let's practice describing another setting with lots of great detail! Write a pretend postcard to a friend from an imaginary vacation in space. Describe the **sights, sounds, smells, feels, and tastes** around you so your friend can picture your setting in their mind.

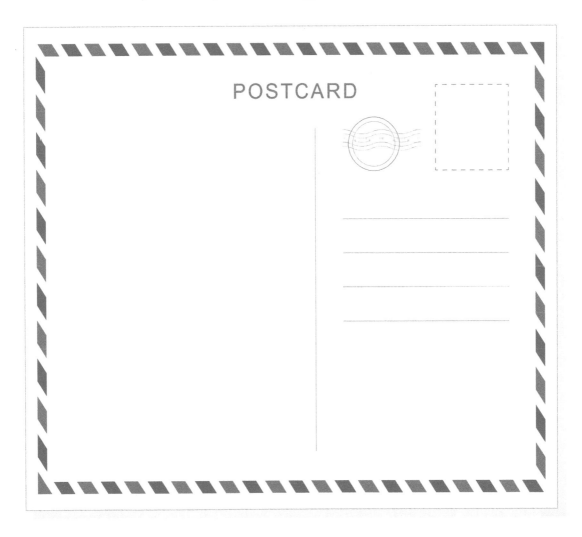

POSTCARD

Ant's World

Practice writing a new setting using lots of fun, descriptive words. Pretend you are an ant in the park. Write about your setting for three minutes without stopping. What do you **see, hear, feel, smell, and taste?** Challenge yourself to use the words *crinkly*, *fresh*, and *damp* in your story.

_____

_____

_____

_____

_____

_____

_____

_____

_____

_____

_____

_____

_____

_____

Writing Secrets

A complete idea is called a **sentence**. Every sentence has a **subject** (the performer) and a verb (the action). You can write AMAZING sentences in your stories with these tips:

Write sentences that are different lengths.

▸ Count the number of words in each sentence of your writing. Are all sentences similar lengths? Try to include both short and long sentences.

▸ Combine two short sentences by adding a comma and the word *and, or, but,* or *so.*

Add variety.

▸ Circle the first word of each sentence. Are too many first words the same? If so, switch them up!

▸ Make your sentences interesting by changing the order of the words. You could write: "The ship twisted and turned as it shot into space" OR "As it shot into space, the ship twisted and turned."

Settings Past and Present

Some stories have more than one setting, like when a story suddenly changes to an earlier time to show the readers something about the past. Give it a try! Write about a superhero who has powers RIGHT NOW. Then, flash back to a time BEFORE they had powers.

Right now: _____

_____

_____

_____

_____

_____

Flash back to a time before: _____

_____

_____

_____

_____

_____

I'm Upside Down!

Different characters notice different things about their setting. This is part of their point of view. Practice writing a setting from a different point of view. Imagine your current setting is upside down! Flip this book upside down to read more.

_____

_____

_____

_____

_____

_____

_____

_____

_____

_____

Write about what it is like to walk around your upside-down world.

Moody Settings

The setting in a story helps create mood. Mood is how a story makes the reader feel. Practice connecting the idea of setting and mood together. Check off the settings that would best create each mood for the reader.

MOOD: **Happy**

- ☐ A party
- ☐ A theme park
- ☐ Outer space
- ☐ The library
- ☐ The ocean

MOOD: **Scared**

- ☐ A dark cave
- ☐ A haunted house
- ☐ An empty field
- ☐ The grocery store
- ☐ The park

MOOD: **Excited**

- ☐ A spaceship
- ☐ A submarine
- ☐ Inside a refrigerator
- ☐ The zoo
- ☐ Your backyard

MOOD: **Sad**

- ☐ A shipwreck
- ☐ An empty house
- ☐ Inside a cage at the zoo
- ☐ The beach
- ☐ The jungle

Spooky Hideout

You stumbled upon a bad guy's hideout! Practice writing a setting with details that create a scary mood. Use your words to paint a picture of the hideout by finishing the sentences.

I slowly entered the dark doorway and saw

_____

_____ .

In the distance, I could hear _____

_____ .

The longer I explored, the more it smelled like

_____ .

The hideout grew darker. I could feel _____

_____ .

I began to see _____ ,

and hear _____ .

Describe That Setting

Adjectives are description words that will help you create interesting settings and strong moods. Check off adjectives you want to use in your writing. If you don't know what a word means, you can look it up in a dictionary or ask an adult. The next time you are writing a story, flip back to this page for some ideas!

☐ Beautiful

☐ Bustling

☐ Calm

☐ Charming

☐ Comfortable

☐ Creepy

☐ Dangerous

☐ Dark

☐ Dull

☐ Gloomy

☐ Happy

☐ Loud

☐ Magical

☐ Mysterious

☐ Quiet

☐ Radiant

☐ Sad

☐ Scary

☐ Stormy

☐ Sunny

Adding the Details: Thoughts, Actions, and Feelings

Understanding a character's thoughts and feelings makes them easy to remember. Describing what a character looks like is important, but favorite characters are the ones readers feel like they KNOW. The prompts in this section will help you share your character's secrets, worries, hopes, and dreams. Remember, a character's perspective is called their point of view.

In these prompts, you will also practice describing your character's actions and behaviors. How do they talk to others? When characters talk to each other in stories, it is called dialogue. Dialogue shows readers a lot about how characters feel.

Last, these prompts will help you think about what makes your character special. For example, you might describe a character who acts brave but feels scared. Or, you might describe a character who acts shy but is a brilliant master spy from another planet. Let's have fun creating characters unlike any other!

Character Thoughts, Feelings, and Actions

In your stories, describe how characters look, feel, and act to make them seem real. Use this page to brainstorm combinations. Mix and match descriptions from the list below to create realistic characters.

THOUGHTS

☐ Brave

☐ Helpful

☐ Horrible

ACTIONS

☐ Quickly

☐ Slowly

☐ Thoughtfully

FEELINGS

☐ Excited

☐ Happy

☐ Nervous

APPEARANCE

☐ Muscular

☐ Sparkly

☐ Terrible

Use this fill-in-the-blank to test your ideas:

My character's thoughts are _____

_____ . However,

they feel _____ .

The character moves _____ and

looks very _____ .

The View from My Window

Use the world around you to practice writing characters that feel real. Look out your window. Who (or what) is the first thing you see? Tell a story from that person's, animal's, bug's, or object's point of view. What are their thoughts? What do they **see, hear, smell, feel, and taste?**

_____

_____

_____

_____

_____

_____

_____

_____

_____

_____

_____

_____

What Are They Thinking?

A character's thoughts, words, feelings, and actions combine to make them a whole person. Create a character by filling in the spaces below.

What is your character thinking?

What does your character say?

_____

_____

_____

What is your character feeling?

What are your character's actions?

_____

_____

_____

Bird Talk

When characters talk in a story, it is called dialogue. Imagine the dialogue between two birds soaring high up in the air. Write what they would say to each other as they zoom above the clouds.

Inspired by Real Life

It can be tricky to make up characters that feel real. Some writers solve this problem by creating characters that are inspired by real life. Give it a try by collecting some ideas here! Choose three people from your life. Think about how you could change them into fictional superheros in a story.

Name of a person I know	New fictional name	Fictional superpower

Writing Secrets

Mark Twain once said, "Don't say the old lady screamed. Bring her on and let her scream." Instead of telling the reader about events that are happening, SHOW them. Here's how:

▶ **Slow down time.** Choose a moment that lasts a few seconds, and stretch it out by describing the sights, sounds, smells, feels, and tastes.

▶ **Add SIMILES to your writing.** A **simile** uses the word *like* or *as* to compare two things that are different. SHOW what a character looks like by saying their eyes are *like* the blue sea or their hair is *as* yellow *as* straw.

▶ **Try describing things with three adjectives** separated by commas. For example: She was wild, strong, and fierce.

▶ **Add onomatopoeias.** An **onomatopoeia** is a word that makes a sound. *Boom! Pow!* and *Bang!* are all examples.

Slow down Time

Now it is your turn to practice showing readers what is happening in lots of detail. Imagine you are in a rocket about to take off from Earth. Write the scene in SLOOOOWWWW motion by describing the **sights, sounds, smells, and feels** of the moment.

_____

_____

_____

_____

_____

_____

_____

_____

_____

_____

_____

_____

Strong Descriptive Words

Sometimes, two words mean almost the same thing, but one of the words is more interesting or more descriptive. You can think of that word as the stronger word, while the other one is weaker. For example, *tired* and *drowsy* mean the same thing, but *drowsy* is more descriptive.

Practice using strong words to describe how a character feels. Replace simple words with stronger words. Check off your favorite strong word in each list.

REPLACE *HAPPY* WITH

☐ cheery

☐ delighted

☐ jolly

☐ lighthearted

REPLACE *SAD* WITH

☐ downhearted

☐ miserable

☐ sorrowful

☐ unhappy

REPLACE *EXCITED* WITH

☐ electrified

☐ elevated

☐ energized

☐ thrilled

REPLACE *SCARED* WITH

☐ alarmed

☐ fearful

☐ horrified

☐ terrified

There Once Was a Wizard

Put everything you've learned about describing realistic characters into action! Tell the story of a powerful wizard who is afraid of his own powers. What does he do? What are his thoughts? How does he feel? Challenge yourself to use strong words and detailed sentences to describe the wizard. Feel free to add an animal sidekick for fun.

_____

_____

_____

_____

_____

_____

_____

_____

_____

_____

_____

My Ideas

Get creative—write, draw, and paste ideas here!

PART 3

In Conclusion

This is the end, my friend. It's time to write a satisfying, magical ending for your story. You will also learn how to edit your writing so readers can focus on your ideas, not your misspelling of the word ~~broccoli~~ broccoli. You've got this!

Make the End Your Friend

Writing the ending of a story is a special gift. It lets you decide how the journey ends for your characters. You can even give hints about how characters' lives will continue after your story is over.

Great endings make readers feel a lot of emotions. Most of all, they leave readers feeling satisfied. The prompts in this section will help you practice showing how the problem of the story is solved. You'll explore ways to show how the character changed or what they learned during the story.

Inspiring Endings

Great story endings show how a character has changed and how the problem of the story was solved. Noticing endings that other writers have written can be a fun way to get inspired.

Write about the endings of two of your favorite books or movies. As you finish your story, look back at this chart for inspiration. Never copy another writer's work. Instead, use their words as an example to help create your own.

FAVORITE BOOKS OR MOVIES	DESCRIBE THE ENDING
1.	
2.	

Resolving Conflict

Now, let's practice writing endings for different stories. Remember, in the beginning of a story, a conflict is introduced. By the end of a story, that conflict should be resolved. Try resolving a few conflicts here! How would each story end?

PROBLEM	RESOLUTION
Miguel didn't make his school's basketball team.	
A homesick alien is stuck on planet Earth.	
Ava walked into her room and found her stuffed animals talking.	

Sloth Solutions

Sometimes, authors end their stories by showing how a character changed. Give it a try! Imagine a sloth who is lonely and shy. She decides to make friends with the moths living in her fur. (Did you know some moth species live in sloths' fur?) How does she change? Write an ending to the sloth's story.

_____

_____

_____

_____

_____

_____

_____

_____

_____

_____

_____

My Ending, My Way

Stories can end in many different ways. The way a story ends can change how the reader feels. Have you ever watched a movie or read a book and wished it could have ended differently? Try rewriting the ending. See where it takes you!

_____

_____

_____

_____

_____

_____

_____

_____

_____

_____

_____

_____

_____

Was It a Happy Ending?

There are a million ways that the problem in a story can be solved at the end. Some endings make readers feel happy. Others might make them feel sad or surprised.

Imagine you are a time traveler who gets stuck in the future. You're looking for a portal that will bring you home. Write three different endings to make your reader feel different emotions.

Happy Ending: _____

_____

_____

_____

Sad Ending: _____

_____

_____

_____

Surprise Ending: _____

_____

_____

_____

Let's Edit!

Everyone makes mistakes, even famous authors. One of the most important steps to writing a great story is checking your work. Checking for mistakes is called **editing**. Making your ideas stronger is called **revising**. The best way to edit and revise is to read your writing out loud.

    The prompts in this section will show you some great tricks for checking your work. You will explore the power of punctuation, capitalization, and spelling. Grab your pencil and eraser and let's get to work!

The Power of Punctuation

When you are reading your stories to edit and revise, pay attention to punctuation. Punctuation can help you show emotion and add detail to your writing. Have fun with punctuation! Challenge yourself to write a story that includes:

- ☐ three descriptive words written in a list and separated by commas. For example, the beast was tall, hairy, and loud.

- ☐ at least one **ellipsis** . . . three dots, separated by spaces, that show a DRAMATIC pause.

- ☐ at least one exclamation point to show excitement!

- ☐ at least one question mark.

_____

_____

_____

_____

_____

_____

_____

_____

Editing the Newspaper

Let's have some fun editing! *The Smalltown Times* is about to print their newspaper. It's full of mistakes! Cross out errors and make corrections. Just like when you are checking your own work, be sure to check punctuation and capitalization.

THE SMALLTOWN TIMES

TOP STORY! robots have been spotted in smalltown. Witnesses claim the robots were having a picnic in farmer brown's cow fields. their meal included apples stolen from Farmer brown's orchard and Corn stolen from his crops

LOCAL EVENTS:
attention all cats! This weekend is the second annual cat party All kittens cats and cat friends are invited. wet and dry food will be served. Dogs will be turned away at the door

ANNOUNCEMENT:
smalltown is trying to set the world record for most kids skateboarding down a ramp at the same time. If you would like to participate, bring your helmet elbow pads and knee pads to town hall this saturday.

FLIP THE PAGE TO CHECK YOUR WORK! ▶

THE SMALLTOWN TIMES

TOP STORY! Robots have been spotted in Smalltown. Witnesses claim the robots were having a picnic in Farmer Brown's cow fields. Their meal included apples stolen from Farmer Brown's orchard and corn stolen from his crops.

LOCAL EVENTS:
Attention all cats! This weekend is the second-annual Cat Party. All kittens, cats, and cat friends are invited. Wet and dry food will be served. Dogs will be turned away at the door.

ANNOUNCEMENT:
Smalltown is trying to set the world record for the most kids skateboarding down a ramp at the same time. If you would like to participate, bring your helmet, elbow pads, and knee pads to Town Hall this Saturday.

In the Land of Capital Letters

When you edit your work, pay attention to capitalization. Capital letters can make a big impact, and this prompt will prove it to you! Imagine a land WHERE EVERYTHING IS CAPITALIZED. Write a story in all capital letters. Then, imagine a land where everything is lowercase. Write a new story in all lowercase letters (even at the start of your sentences!). How does the story change?

THE LAND OF CAPITAL LETTERS:

_____

_____

_____

_____

_____

the land of lowercase letters:

_____

_____

_____

_____

_____

Writing Secrets

Become a homonym superhero! **Homonyms** are words that sound the same but have different meanings. Edit your writing and make sure you are using the right words.

THERE is a place.

THEIR means they own it.

THEY'RE means they are.

TO means in the direction of. Sometimes **TO** is used as part of a verb (like *to run* or *to dance*).

TOO means also or very.

TWO is a number.

YOUR means you own it.

YOU'RE means you are.

OUR means we own it.

ARE is a form of the verb *to be*.

Astronaut Edits

Write a story about an astronaut living in space. Describe the **sights, sounds, smells, feels, and tastes** the astronaut experiences. Now, practice your editing and revising super skills! Read the story you just wrote. Cross out or erase your mistakes. Pay close attention to punctuation, capitalization, and spelling. Next, look at the descriptive words you used. Can you revise them to make them more powerful?

_____

_____

_____

_____

_____

_____

_____

_____

_____

_____

_____

Putting It All Together

You've learned TONS about how to write brilliant beginnings, puzzling plots, and crafty characters. Tie it all together. Brainstorm a story about a person from history who comes to visit you at school. What would you do? How would your story end? These ideas will be waiting here the next time you're ready to start a new story.

BEGINNING: _____

_____

_____

_____

MIDDLE: _____

_____

_____

_____

END: _____

_____

_____

_____

Terrific Topics

Now that you're an author, check off topics that you'd like to write about in the future. You'll have some great ideas lined up for many stories to come.

- ☐ A time portal at school
- ☐ Animals in the wild
- ☐ Dinosaurs coming back to life
- ☐ Food that comes to life
- ☐ Outer space adventures
- ☐ People from history
- ☐ Pets and their adventures

- ☐ Sports adventures
- ☐ Stories inspired by your favorite songs
- ☐ Superheroes with surprising flaws
- ☐ Trees that talk
- ☐ Underwater caves
- ☐ Villains who turn good

List some of your own ideas:

▶ _____

▶ _____

▶ _____

▶ _____

My Ideas

Get creative—write, draw, and paste ideas here!

Keep Writing!

Congratulations! You have written an entire book of stories and ideas to build on, read, and celebrate for years to come. You are an author!

Everyone sees the world differently. Keep telling stories from your special point of view. No story is too wild or too silly. Start a new notebook or journal to store ideas, write stories, and practice the writing skills you've learned from this book. Collect pictures, quotes, words, and ideas. Brainstorm, freewrite, plot stories, edit, and revise. Remember that mistakes are your greatest teachers. The key is to keep writing and have fun.

Write about your dreams, your wishes, your pets, and the people in your community. Inspiration is all around you. Write about your own experiences, and throw in some twists and turns. Remember that stories can take you anywhere. Keep bringing magical stories to life!

Glossary

action lead: When a story starts in the middle of an event

adjective: A word that describes a person, place, animal, or thing. *Big*, *fast*, and *thoughtful* are examples of adjectives.

conflict: The problem that happens in a story

dialogue: A conversation between two or more characters in a book or movie

editing: Checking writing for mistakes and correcting them. Editing usually happens after the first draft of a story is written.

ellipsis: A punctuation mark. Three dots that show a dramatic pause.

freewriting: When a person writes without stopping for a certain amount of time (usually a few minutes) without worrying about spelling or grammar

hero: The main character in a story

homonym: A word that sounds the same as another word but is spelled differently and has a different meaning. *There* and *their* are examples of homonyms.

mood: The way a story makes a reader feel

narrative writing: Writing that connects ideas in order to tell a story. Narratives usually have a beginning, middle, and end.

noun: A word that names a person, place, or thing. *Baseball, girl,* and *teacher* are examples of nouns.

onomatopoeia: A word that sounds like a sound and names a sound. *Buzz* is an example of onomatopoeia.

plot: The series of events that make up a story. The events in a plot build from the beginning, to the middle, the turning point, and the end.

point of view: The perspective of the person who is telling a story. When someone tells a story through their experiences, the story is from their point of view.

revising: Making changes to writing to express stronger ideas or stories. Revising usually happens after a first draft of a story is written.

sentence: A group of words that form a complete thought

setting: When and where a story takes place

simile: Comparing two things using the words *like* or *as.* The alien's skin was as *slimy as a slug* is an example of a simile.

subject: The person or thing that a sentence is about; the person or thing doing the action in the sentence

tension: The feeling of wonder or worry about what will happen next in a story

theme: The message of a story, which is always a complete idea. *Be yourself* is an example of a theme.

turning point: The moment in the story when an important change happens. The turning point usually happens in the middle of the story.

verb: A word that describes an action. *Run, jump*, and *fly* are examples of verbs.

villain: A character in a story who is against the hero

Resources

You have worked very hard to strengthen your writing skills. Continue writing using these awesome tools.

MagneticPoetry.com is great if you want to have fun playing with words. This website gives users words to click and drag into endless combinations.

Read. Write. Think. has interactive organizers young writers can use to map stories. You can find them at ReadWriteThink.org.

Scholastic Story Starters gives kids fun writing prompts. Check them out at Scholastic.com/teachers/story-starters/index. You can choose a subject, a format, and get started!

StoryJumper.com allows young writers to create books, share them, and even publish them.

About the Author

 **EMILY AIERSTOK** is a writer and middle school English language arts teacher from the Capital Region of upstate New York. She received her master's degree in English education from the University of Albany. Her passion is coming up with engaging curricula that help kids fall in love with reading and writing. She shares her ideas and inspiration with other educators through her Instagram account and blog, *Read it. Write it. Learn it.* Emily loves traveling, designing, writing, and most of all, spending time with her family and friends. She has been teaching for more than twenty years. You can follow her on Instagram at @readitwriteitlearnit.

My About the Author

Write your own About the Author page. Include where you go to school, your interests, where you live, and who's in your family. You can even add a photo of yourself!

_____

_____

_____

_____

_____

_____

_____

_____

_____

Acknowledgments

Our imaginations have the power to take us anywhere. My imagination was sparked early by my parents. It is alive and well because of my three children, Ava, Max, and Cam. To them: Thank you for keeping my storytelling alive. You will always be the heart behind my work. Thank you to my husband, Kevin, for listening to my ideas and, most important, for believing that I can accomplish things that seem bigger than me. Thank you to Evie, Lilah, and Graham for sharing your creativity with me. You are authors, too. Thank you to my editor, Maxine Marshall, for your encouragement and to Rakhshan Rizwan for finding me the perfect book. Finally, thank you to my students for inspiring me to be a better human. You give me hope.

My Acknowledgments

Who would you like to thank for inspiring and supporting
your writing? Write your acknowledgments here.

_____

_____

_____

_____

_____

_____

_____

_____

_____

_____

_____

_____

_____

_____

_____

_____

CPSIA information can be obtained
at www.ICGtesting.com
Printed in the USA
JSHW050243031122
32384JS00011B/29

9 781685 395711